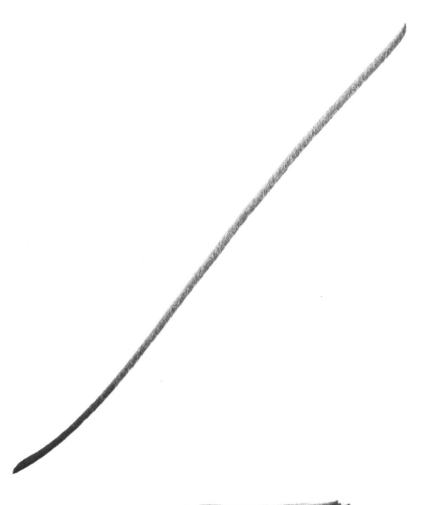

The United States

Idaho

Paul Joseph
ABDO & Daughters

visit us at
www.abdopub.com

Published by Abdo & Daughters, 4940 Viking Drive, Suite 622, Edina, Minnesota 55435.
Copyright © 1998 by Abdo Consulting Group, Inc., Pentagon Tower, P.O. Box 36036, Minneapolis, Minnesota 55435 USA. International copyrights reserved in all countries. No part of this book may be reproduced in any form without written permission from the publisher.

Printed in the United States.

Cover and Interior Photo credits: Peter Arnold, Inc., Super Stock

Edited by Lori Kinstad Pupeza
Contributing editor Brooke Henderson
Special thanks to our Checkerboard Kids—Stephanie McKenna, Jack Ward, Francesca Tuminelly

All statistics taken from the 1990 census; The Rand McNally Discovery Atlas of The United States. Other sources: Compton's Encyclopedia, 1997; *Idaho*, Heinrichs, Children's Press, Chicago, 1989.

Library of Congress Cataloging-in-Publication Data

Joseph, Paul, 1970-
    Idaho/Paul Joseph.
    p.   cm. -- (The United States)
    Includes index.
    Summary: Examines the geography, history, natural resources, people, and sports of Idaho.
    ISBN 1-56239-857-1
    1. Idaho--Juvenile literature. [1. Idaho.]   I. Title. II. Series: United States (series)
    F746.3.J67   1998
    979.6--DC21   97-6681
                                                  CIP
                                                  AC

Contents

Welcome to Idaho

Idaho's odd shape looks something like a logger's boot. The reason for the shape is because Idaho is what remained after the six states around it made their **borders**.

Idaho is located in the Northwest. Its borders include Canada to the north, Oregon and Washington to the west, Montana and Wyoming to the east, and Nevada and Utah to the south.

The beautiful state of Idaho has towering mountains, long, swift rivers, steep waterfalls, evergreen forests, and unbelievable canyons. It is no wonder that more than six million people visit Idaho each year. Because of its beauty, it is nicknamed the Gem State.

Although the state of Idaho is thinly populated, it is still a very important state. There are a lot of **natural**

resources. It has been the leading **producer** of silver, zinc, lead, and wood. Farming is the biggest money maker in Idaho. Idaho potatoes are nationally famous. Hay, sugar beets, and wheat are other **crops** grown there.

Tourists enjoy the national parks, the wonderful mountain ski resorts, the hunting, and the fishing.

Iron Creek in the Sawtooth Mountains of Idaho.

Fast Facts

IDAHO

Capital and largest city
Boise (125,738 people)
Area
82,413 square miles
(213,449 sq km)
Population
1,011,986 people
Rank: 42nd
Statehood
July 3, 1890
(43rd state admitted)
Principal river
Snake River
Highest point
Borah Peak;
12,662 feet (3,859 m)
Motto
Esto perpetua
(Let it be perpetual)
Song
"Here We Have Idaho"
Famous People
Moses Alexander, William
Borah, Gutzon Borglum, Frank
Church, Ezra Pound

*S*tate Flag

*I*daho Syringa

*M*ountain Bluebird

*W*hite Pine

About Idaho

The Gem State

Detail area

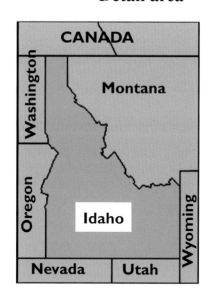

Idaho's abbreviation

Borders: west (Washington, Oregon), north (Canada), east (Montana, Wyoming), south (Nevada, Utah)

Nature's Treasures

Idaho has a variety of **natural resources**. Farmers can grow a lot of **crops** in the rich soil of Idaho's valleys. The land is also good for **cattle** and sheep to **graze**.

Much of the state of Idaho is forest. There are mainly white pine, yellow pine, red cedar, fir, and spruce trees.

Other resources include **minerals** in the earth and beautiful recreation areas. Rivers and mountains add to Idaho's natural beauty. **Tourists** come from all over to see the beauty of Idaho in both winter and summer months.

The weather is also a treasure. In the southern part of the state the summers are dry and very warm. The winters can have snow one day and be warm the next. In the northern part of Idaho, the winters can be long and severe. Summers, though, are very nice.

Idaho's land is mostly forest.

Beginnings

The first people to live in Idaho were two major **Native American** tribes. The Nez Percé occupied the north. The southern part of Idaho was occupied by the Shoshone or Snake.

In 1805, Meriweather Lewis and William Clark became the first non-Native Americans to explore the region. After Lewis and Clark came, there was a rush of fur trappers into the area.

In the 1800s, **European** settlers were taking over the land. There were many wars between the Native Americans and the settlers.

After the discovery of gold in 1860, the **population** grew in Idaho. By 1863, about 15,000 people had come to Idaho to look for gold.

In 1890, Idaho was admitted to the Union as the 43rd state. Boise became the capital.

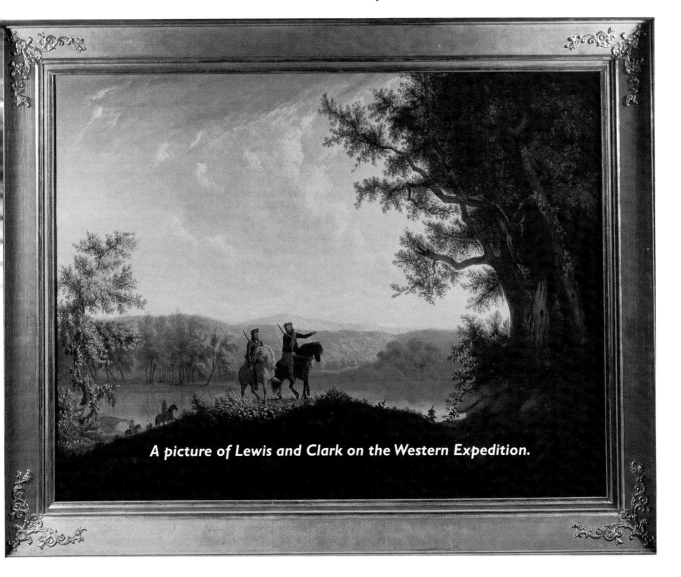

A picture of Lewis and Clark on the Western Expedition.

B.C. to 1800

Early Land and People

 Many thousands of years ago cave men and dinosaurs roamed Idaho.

 During the Ice Age, Idaho was covered in glaciers and ice.

 After the Ice Age, the glaciers melted and the area was filled with mountains, rivers, lakes, and forests.

 The first known people to occupy Idaho were the Nez Percé who occupied northern Idaho and the Shoshone or Snake who occupied the south.

12

Idaho
BC to 1800

1800s

Explorers, Settlers, and Miners

 1805: Lewis and Clark enter Idaho.

 1819: Spain gives up claim of territory, which includes Idaho.

 1860: Gold is discovered on Orofino Creek.

 1861: Gold strikes made on Salmon and Boise rivers.

Idaho
1800s

1890 to Now

Statehood and Beyond

1890: Idaho becomes 43rd state on July 3. Boise is named the capital.

1950: **Native Americans** are given full citizenship.

1965: The Nez Percé National Historical Park is established.

1990: Idaho celebrates 100 years of being part of the United States of America.

17

Idaho's People

There are only a little over one million people that live in the state of Idaho. There are 41 states that are larger than Idaho. The **population** continues to grow, and many **tourists** visit this beautiful state each year.

Native Americans were the first people to live on Idaho's land. Today, it is mainly Anglos that make up the state. Anglo people came from England, Germany, Italy, Russia, and other countries in Europe.

Native Americans make up a small amount of people in Idaho. Most live on **reservations**. Along with Native Americans, Japanese, African Americans, and Hispanics make up less than five percent of Idaho's population.

There are many notable people of Idaho. The state's most famous **politician** was Senator William E. Borah. Borah Peak, the highest point in Idaho, was named after him. Cecil D. Andrus was elected governor of Idaho in

1970 and served until 1977. Andrus loved the **environment**. He fought to keep **nuclear plants** out of the state of Idaho.

Lana Turner was born in Wallace, Idaho. She was a great actress. She starred in "Ziegfeld Girl" and "The Postman Always Rings Twice."

Harmon Killebrew was born in Payette, Idaho. Killebrew was a great home run hitter for the Washington Senators and Minnesota Twins. He finished his career with the Kansas City Royals. Killebrew was inducted into the Baseball Hall of Fame in 1984.

Harmon Killebrew

Lana Turner

Splendid Cities

Idaho is a thinly **populated** state. Only Ada County has a population of more than 100,000 people.

Boise is both the capital and the largest city. Around 125,000 people live there. Boise is a trade and **agriculture** center located in the southwest of the state. It has two state and four city parks.

Pocatello is the second largest city. It is in the southeast part of the state. Pocatello is a railroad and trade center. It is also the home to Idaho State University.

Idaho Falls is a beautiful city on the upper Snake River. It is noted for its farming products. Lewiston, in northern Idaho, is a major **manufacturer** of lumber and wood products.

Lewiston

Boise

Idaho Falls

Pocatello

20

The State Capitol, in Boise, Idaho.

Idaho's Land

Idaho's area is 82,413 square miles (213,449 sq km) including 1,152 square miles (2,984 sq km) of water surface. This mountainous state is divided into four different regions: the Northern Rockies, the Middle Rockies, the Columbia Plateau, and the Great Basin.

The Northern Rockies is the largest region and covers most of the northern half of the state. This region has many ranges of mountains. It also has many rivers. The highest point in the state, Borah Peak, is in this region.

The Middle Rockies is the region on the southeastern **border** of the state. There are two outer mountain ranges in this area. The Tetons, which extend into Wyoming, and the Wasatch, which is mainly in Utah.

The Columbia Plateau follows the Snake River through southern Idaho and then northward along the western **border**. This region has Idaho's lowest point. The valley of the Snake River drops to 710 feet (216 m).

The Great Basin is a triangle-shaped region in the south between the Middle Rockies and the Columbia Plateau. It is mainly desert plains with some mountains.

The Grand Teton mountain range.

Idaho at Play

Idaho's sunshine, warmth, rivers, and beautiful land bring thousands of people to this state in the summer. In the winter thousands come to the resorts of Idaho for its great mountain skiing.

There are more than 30,000 acres of Yellowstone National Park in eastern Idaho. Yellowstone is one of the most beautiful parks in the nation.

Sun Valley was the first major ski resort in the United States. It was developed in 1936 and today is still one of the most popular year-round resorts. In the winter, people ski. In the summer, people hike, mountain bike, and enjoy the beauty.

The wonderful lake cities of Coeur d' Alene and Sandpoint and the incredible Nez Percé National Historical Park attract people to the northern part of Idaho.

The people of Idaho and **tourists** who visit also enjoy big-game hunting, trout fishing, and camping.

Wildlife viewing in Yellowstone Park, Idaho.

Idaho at Work

The people of Idaho must work to make money. Many of the jobs deal with **tourism** and service. Service is cooking and serving food, working in stores, hotels, or restaurants, and doing many other service jobs.

A lot of people in Idaho are farmers, **miners**, and **manufacturers**. Farming provides a major source of income for the state and employs about 13 percent of the people. Idaho is the leading state in the **production** of potatoes. Wheat, sugar beets, hay, and barley also rank high in production. The livestock raised are **cattle**, sheep, and pigs.

Minerals have added to Idaho's wealth. The state is one of the leading producers of silver, lead, and zinc. Rock, sand, and gravel are also produced.

There is no single large **manufacturing** center in Idaho, rather many small ones. The most important is the manufacturing of lumber and wood products.

Second is the processing of food products such as meat, butter, fruits and vegetables.

Idaho began as a mining state and today is known for its beauty, resorts, and wonderful climate. The Gem State is a great place to visit, live, work, and play.

An Idaho potato farmer.

Fun Facts

•The highest point in Idaho is Borah Peak and it is very tall. It is 12,662 feet (3,859 meters). The lowest area in the state is near the Snake River. It is only 710 feet (216 meters).

•Idaho is very large in land size. Only 12 other states are bigger than Idaho. Idaho's land covers 82,413 square miles (213,449 square kilometers). In **population**, however, Idaho is small. There are 41 states larger than Idaho in population.

•At one point Idaho was going to be named Montana, which means "mountainous" in Spanish. However, people wanted the name to come from Indian words. Some say that the state got its name Idaho because it sounded like "Indian." Others say that it was a Shoshone Indian term "E-dah-how" which was made into Idaho. The term "E-dah-how" means: "It is sunup!"

•The Shoshone Falls of the Snake River has a rim nearly 1,000 feet (305 m) wide. These falls fall 212 feet (65 m). When the sun is out a huge rainbow forms from the falls.

The Snake River in Idaho.

Glossary

Agriculture: another name for farming.

Border: neighboring states, countries, or waters.

Cattle: farm animals such as cows, bulls, and oxen.

Crops: what farmers grow on their farm to either eat or sell or do both.

Environment: the natural area of land, such as mountains, rivers, valleys.

European: people who originally come from countries in Europe such as England, Germany, Italy, etc.

Graze: animals eating grass.

Manufacture: to make things by machine in a factory.

Minerals: things found in the earth, such as rock, diamonds, coal, etc.

Miners: people who work underground to get minerals.

Native Americans: the first people who were born and occupied North America.

Natural resources: found in nature that is not made by people. Such as rock, sand, water, etc.

Politician: an elected official that makes laws for the city, county, state, or country.

Population: the number of people living in an area.

Produce: to make.

Reservations: an area of land where Native Americans live, work, and have their own laws.

Tourism: an industry that serves people who are traveling for pleasure, and visiting places of interest.

Tourists: people who travel for pleasure.

Internet Sites

Idaho Wilderness
http://www.wild-eyed.org
Information on wilderness areas, roadless areas, conservation politics, Idaho's endangered species, and wolves.

Scenic Idaho
http://www.Scenic-Idaho.com
Places to go and things to do in the Heart of Idaho: Central Idaho; for the outdoor enthusiast.

Idaho Department of Commerce
http://www.idoc.state.id.us
An attractive business atmosphere, exceptional quality of life, limitless recreation opportunities and warm family environment make Idaho a truly unique place.

These sites are subject to change. Go to your favorite search engine and type in Idaho for more sites.

PASS IT ON

Tell Others Something Special About Your State

To educate readers around the country, pass on interesting tips, places to see, history, and little unknown facts about the state you live in. We want to hear from you!

To get posted on ABDO & Daughters website E-mail us at "mystate@abdopub.com"

Index